Engineering Feats

FAST Telescope

Marty Gitlin

Mitchell Lane
PUBLISHERS

2001 SW 31st Avenue
Hallandale, FL 33009
www.mitchelllane.com

Printing   1   2   3   4   5   6   7   8

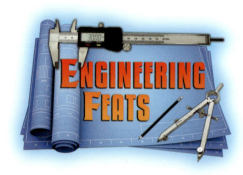

Designer: Sharon Beck
Editor: Jim Whiting

Library of Congress Cataloging-in-Publication Data
Names: Gitlin, Marty, author.
Title: The FAST telescope / by Marty Gitlin.
Description: Hallandale, FL : Mitchell Lane Publishers, [2018] | Series: Engineering feats | FAST
    stands for Five-hundred-meter Aperture Spherical Telescope. | Audience: Grades 4 to 6. | Includes
    bibliographical references and index.
Identifiers: LCCN 2017046722 | ISBN 9781680201642 (library bound)
Subjects: LCSH: Radio telescopes—Juvenile literature. | Radio telescopes—China—Juvenile
    literature. | Radio astronomy—Juvenile literature. | Very long baseline interferometry—Juvenile
    literature. | CYAC: Telescopes.
Classification: LCC QB479.2 .G58 2018 | DDC 522/.682—dc23
LC record available at https://lccn.loc.gov/2017046722

eBook ISBN: 9-781-6802-0165-9

CONTENTS

Words in **bold** throughout can be found in the Glossary.

1
Big Hope for a Big Telescope

The universe is a mystery. There are a million questions for every answer. And one question has seemingly been asked more than any other: Is there life on other planets?

Nobody knows for sure. Experts believe it is probable. At least 200 billion **galaxies** exist and each one of them has many planets. So how likely is it that Earth is the only one with living beings? Not very.

Yet there is no proof. The truth remains unknown. For centuries, scientists have been unable to find out. But just maybe they will now.

The date was September 25, 2016, in the remote Guizhou Province of southeast China. That is when the FAST telescope first opened its eyes. That is when the marvel of engineering started studying the universe. That is when it began detecting images and sounds beyond what anyone had ever been seen or heard.

Its full name is the Five-Hundred-Meter **Aperture** Spherical Telescope. It is the world's largest radio telescope. According to the National Radio **Astronomy** Observatory, "Radio telescopes collect weak radio light waves, bring them to a focus, amplify them and make them available for analysis. . . . Naturally occurring radio waves are extremely weak by the time they reach us from space. A cell phone signal is a billion billion times more powerful than the cosmic waves our telescopes detect."[1]

Its field of vision is more than twice that of anything built before it. Its gigantic dish is 500 meters (1,640 feet) in diameter. Its area is

The enormity of the FAST Telescope, which is 500 meters in diameter, is shown in this aerial shot. The photo was taken the day before the structure was completed and put into use.

the same size as 30 soccer fields. A total of 4,450 panels receive signals from billions of miles away in space.

The new marvel works to hear signals from distant galaxies. It will help store the memory of radio waves known as **pulsars**. It will probe **gravitational waves**. It will seek out dark matter. That is previously unexplored space that makes up most of the universe.[2]

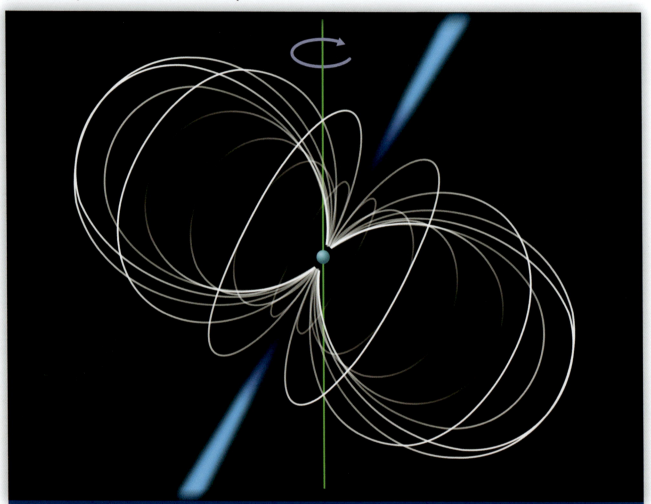

Schematic view of a pulsar. It is centered on a neutron star, the dot in the center. A neutron star is what remains of a dying star. It is only about 10 miles in diameter and so dense that a teaspoon of matter weighs a billion tons. As it quickly rotates on its axis (the vertical green line), it produces an incredibly strong magnetic field (the white circles). This magnetic field greatly accelerates particles to produce radio waves (the two blue lines). FAST and other radio telescopes seek to detect these radio waves.

Most important, it will listen for signals from alien beings. Three potentially life-friendly planets were recently discovered outside our solar system. That has sparked interest again in whether intelligent life exists elsewhere.[3]

FAST FACT ✏

Scientists now know the universe is growing. But what is it growing into? Does it have an edge? Is there something beyond the known universe? Nobody knows for sure. But attempts have been made to find out if the universe is a sphere. Scientists believe it might curve back on itself. That means someone traveling in one direction would eventually return to the starting point.[4]

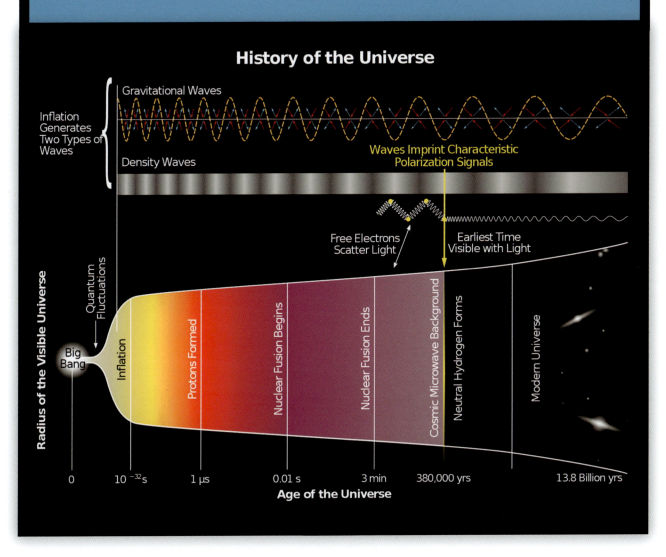

History of the Universe

Gravitational Waves

Inflation Generates Two Types of Waves

Density Waves

Waves Imprint Characteristic Polarization Signals

Free Electrons Scatter Light

Earliest Time Visible with Light

Radius of the Visible Universe

Quantum Fluctuations

Big Bang

Inflation

Protons Formed

Nuclear Fusion Begins

Nuclear Fusion Ends

Cosmic Microwave Background

Neutral Hydrogen Forms

Modern Universe

| 0 | 10^{-32} s | 1 μs | 0.01 s | 3 min | 380,000 yrs | 13.8 Billion yrs |

Age of the Universe

The extent of the universe remains unknown. People wonder if it ever ends. Scientists are certain that it continues to expand.

Questions like these may never be answered. However, the telescope might be able to answer another question that has puzzled humans for as long as they have existed: How did the universe begin?

The answer might be found in pulsars and gravitational waves. They can shed light on how galaxies evolved.

How much of it can the telescope hear? There is no way to know yet. The answer lies in its triangular aluminum panels. They can be adjusted to search for signals in various parts of the cosmos. A mesh of steel cables pushes and pulls them in different directions. That is a feature that makes the FAST Telescope special.[5]

The cable net of the telescope is seen in this image taken during construction of the telescope construction in July, 2015.

The top photo shows the installation of the first panel to the reflector of the telescope in August, 2015. The bottom photo shows the nearly completed installation 11 months later.

We cannot be sure it will find what it seeks. It is possible that there is no life on other planets. Or that beings live beyond what FAST is capable of detecting.

However, the FAST telescope does greatly increase the chances of discovering **alien** life forms if they do exist. Peng Bo of the National Astronomical Observatories Radio Astronomy Technology Laboratory in Beijing, China, believes that it is far more likely to make such discoveries than other telescopes. "FAST's potential to discover an alien civilization will be 5 to 10 (times) that of current equipment, as it can see farther and darker planets,"[6] he said.

Excitement over the amazing telescope has helped to energize the Chinese space program. China launched its unmanned Tiangong-2 space lab into Earth orbit in 2016. It plans on building a 20-ton space station and sending an astronaut to the moon. It hopes to land a robotic probe on Mars by 2020.

The FAST telescope could aid the Chinese in their efforts. It could track some of those missions. But it has its limits. It is unable to project where comets and asteroids are heading in the sky. That means it cannot warn people if they are hurtling toward Earth.

That worries Douglas Vakoch. He is the president of METI (Messaging Extraterrestrial Intelligence) International. The organization's goal is to learn about the

FAST FACT

One sound the FAST Telescope might detect is a fast radio burst (FRB). That is a radio pulse lasting much less than one second. The FRB was discovered by college professor Duncan Lorimer and his student David Narkovic in 2007. Other bursts have since been recorded. Their origin remains a mystery. It is hoped that FAST will provide the answer.[7]

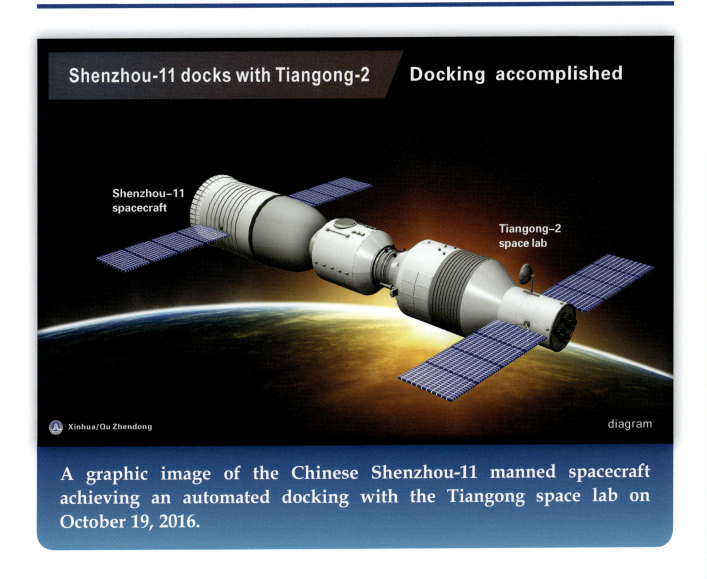

Shenzhou-11 docks with Tiangong-2   Docking accomplished

Shenzhou-11
spacecraft

Tiangong-2
space lab

Xinhua/Qu Zhendong   diagram

A graphic image of the Chinese Shenzhou-11 manned spacecraft achieving an automated docking with the Tiangong space lab on October 19, 2016.

possible existence of living beings on other planets. "FAST may help explain the origin of the universe and the structure of the cosmos, but it won't provide warning of earth-bound asteroids that can destroy human civilization,"[8] Vakoch said. What it can do is exciting enough. So is the way in which the telescope was planned and designed. It is indeed an engineering marvel!

Birth of a Marvel

The seeds of FAST were planted more than two decades ago. A project called the Square Kilometer Array (SKA) had been proposed in 1993. The idea behind it was that radio waves received by hundreds of small, widely spaced dishes would provide a wider range and be more powerful than large ones. China wanted to host the SKA and offered to build several dishes in its southeast provinces. Chinese astronomers even researched FAST as a possible SKA dish. Disappointment followed when China was dropped from consideration in 2006. The host countries instead would be South Africa and Australia.

That setback did not stop Chinese scientists. They pushed to build the FAST telescope anyway. They felt that it would excel at searching for alien life. And they figured it would be cheaper.

The government pumped about $180 million into the venture. It was led by astronomer Rendong Nan, who was named chief scientist and engineer of the project in 2008. He needed his skills in both fields to produce the best results.

Nan received his B.S. degree in electronics technology in 1968 and earned a Ph.D. degree in astronomy and astrophysics two decades later. Starting in 1982, he worked as an astronomer for the Chinese Academy of Sciences. He also spent more than six years overseas as a guest professor in Italy, France, England, Canada, the United States, and the Netherlands.[1]

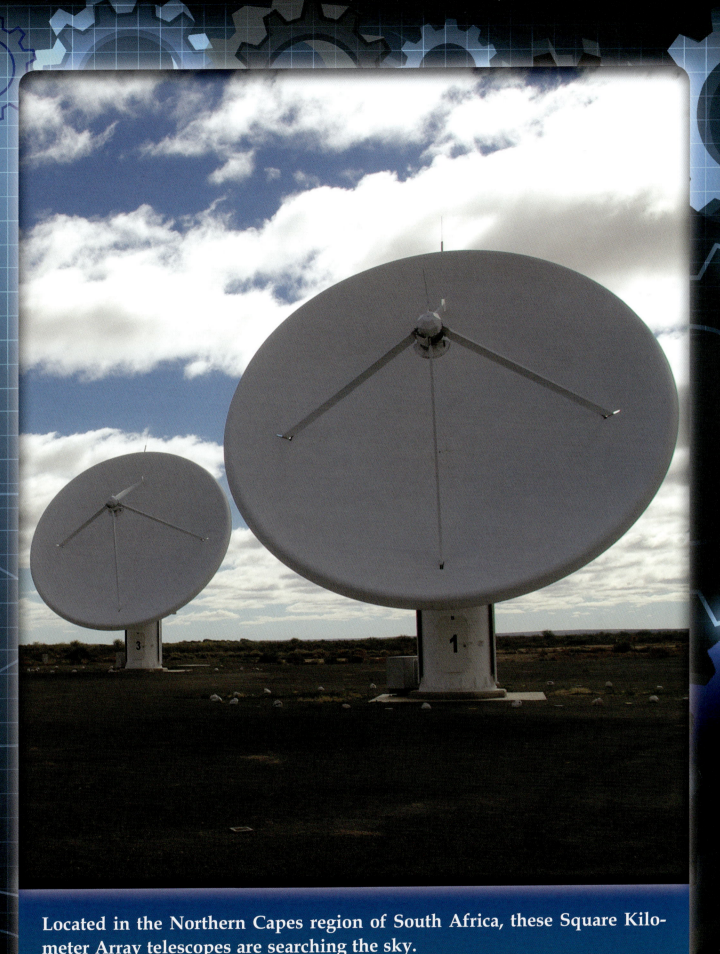

Located in the Northern Capes region of South Africa, these Square Kilometer Array telescopes are searching the sky.

His research for the best site to place the FAST Telescope resulted in 400 potential spots, all in southeast China. It had to be a remote area with no radio **interference**.[2]

Nan eventually chose the Dawodang **Depression**. He recalled hiking into the crater there and seeing a circular view of the sky above. He compared it to being at the bottom of a well.[3] It was an ideal place for the telescope. The mountains surrounding it protected against outside radio interference.

FAST FACT

The spot in which the FAST Telescope was placed has been described as a "karst hollow." A hollow is sunken land. A karst is a type of landscape formed by crumbled rocks such as limestone. About one in four people in the world either lives in or obtains water from karst areas.[4]

The construction site, however, was not ideal. It was hours from the nearest highway, accessible only by rough, narrow roads that wound through tiny villages. Workers built a road linking the crater to the nearest town. They had to carry heavy loads in sizzling hot weather.[5]

The workers had it better than those who lived nearby. The Green Water Village was located at the bottom of the depression. Though it had no electricity, the village housed 12 families and a total of 65 people. They had to move to make room for the telescope. One of the displaced residents was Yang Chaolan. She was angry even though her son planned to open a restaurant in the town where they moved in order to serve Guizhou theme parks. That did not make her feel much better. She had lived in the region her entire life. "I never thought the first time I would move would be to make room for a telescope,"[6] she said.

The karst basin into which the FAST telescope is placed is seen here in the Guizhou Province of China. It had been one of the most remote and quiet spots in the country until tourists arrived.

This April 2009 aerial view shows the site in southeast China where the FAST telescope was constructed. The houses are the Green Water Village, which had to be destroyed and its residents relocated.

More than 9,000 other people were forced to leave their homes to prevent any electronic interference with the telescope's ability to listen for signals. Most people in Guizhou Province have little money. It is one of the poorest regions in the country. They had no choice but to move. Each received less than $2,000 to find a new home.

In addition to Yang Chaolan, other people complained about their forced relocation. About 500 families sued the local government. A man named Lu Zhenglong claimed that his house was destroyed without warning or his consent. He was thankful he was not in the house at the time. "What would have happened if I had been inside?"[7] he asked. A neighbor, also named Lu, expressed his anger when he said, "They've chased us all off to some wasteland and ordered us to live there with no

FAST FACT ✏️

China does not enjoy freedom of the press. What is often told is what the government wants people to hear. The media reported little about the families who were forced out of their homes to make room for the telescope. They boasted instead about how it advanced astronomy in their country.[10]

way to maintain our old standard of living. "For 90 percent of us, basic survival is a problem."[8]

The Chinese government could not ignore the problem. It spent about $269 million in poverty relief funds and bank loans to help relocate the residents. That was more than the total cost of the telescope.[9]

The telescope was modeled after the Arecibo Observatory radio telescope, which was built in 1963 in Puerto Rico and measures 305 meters (1,000 feet) in diameter. They are both built in craters. They are both supported by steel cable screens. The FAST screens hang from supports fixed to the highest points in the limestone.

Most radio telescopes stand tall off the ground. They focus waves from objects in space in line with its axis to a point above the telescope. The dish can be steered and track objects in space as the Earth rotates.

Nan understood that round dishes such as FAST and Arecibo could not be steered. They are stuck to the ground. They must detect waves without focusing on one point.

Arecibo aims at objects in the sky by shifting its platform to catch reflected waves. But that limits what it can observe. And its platform weighs 1.8 million pounds.[11]

Nan had a better idea. It would result in an engineering marvel that could see far more than Arecibo. The FAST Telescope was about to take shape.

3

Bigger and Stronger

It is natural to compare the FAST Telescope with Arecibo. FAST replaced its predecessor as the most powerful in the world. But there really is no comparison. The FAST telescope is not just bigger. It features a larger signal receiving area. It is more flexible. It can gather far more information about the great unknown.

And that is what is most important. The telescope was built to turn the great unknown into the known. A thirst for knowledge is a driving force of humanity.

Di Li understands that. He seeks answers to the mysteries of the universe. He is chief scientist for the National Astronomical Observatories in China. Li believes in gaining knowledge of what exists in deep space. He feels that is critical to moving the world forward. "Exploring the unknown is the nature of mankind, which is as (instinctive) as feeding and clothing ourselves," Li said. "It drives us to a great future."[1]

Construction of the FAST telescope began in 2011. A decision had been made to design it differently than Arecibo. The Arecibo scope aims at objects in space by shifting its platform to catch reflected waves. A complex mirror system in the platform brings those waves into focus. That limits how much sky it can observe. And the platform is simply too heavy.

The FAST team designed a system that pulls as much as 300 meters (985 feet) of the dish into a curve shape. The shape is like the

An aerial view of the construction site of the FAST telescope is shown here about 15 months after the project was launched.

path of something thrown forward in the air that falls back to the ground. It enables the telescope to remain trained on a specific object in space as the Earth rotates. "It's like forming a smaller bowl within a big wok,"[2] Li explained.

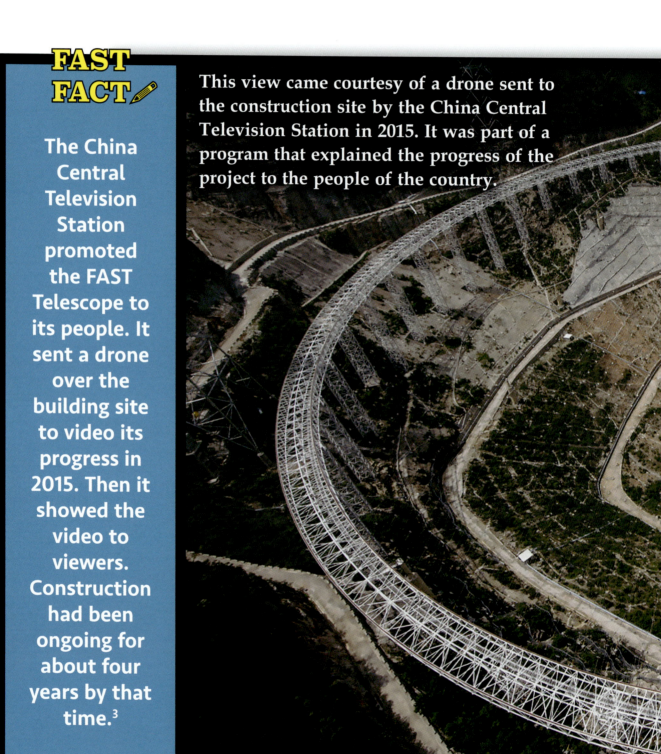

FAST FACT

The China Central Television Station promoted the FAST Telescope to its people. It sent a drone over the building site to video its progress in 2015. Then it showed the video to viewers. Construction had been ongoing for about four years by that time.[3]

This view came courtesy of a drone sent to the construction site by the China Central Television Station in 2015. It was part of a program that explained the progress of the project to the people of the country.

The telescope has more than 2,000 computer-controlled **winches**. They are anchored into rock beneath the dish. They move the part of the dish into a curved position through cables connected to the supports. The winches are relaxed when the round shape of the dish needs to be restored.

Building the telescope that way was not easy. Many challenges awaited the workers. They had to construct a shield to stop radio signals from being sent into space. The outgoing signals would have been many times stronger than those received and would have caused interference.[4]

The support system of the FAST Telescope can be seen in this November, 2015 image of the construction site.

This photo shows the receiver installed at the site where the telescope is being built.

Engineers had to overcome another obstacle. Constantly bending steel cables in opposite directions caused them to break like a paper clip bent back and forth. Nan and his designers came up with a solution. They learned about a cable made in China that resists breaking. It stays together even when it is bent up to two million times. The FAST steel cables are only expected to bend about 300,000 times in 30 years, the entire design life of the telescope.

FAST was almost completed in January, 2016. Most of the 4,450 panels had been placed. There was just one problem. None of its radio receivers were ready. Nan yearned to test the new marvel. So he got

Construction workers put a feedback source cabin for the telescope into place in April, 2016.

creative. He had his team rig up a skinny TV antenna and put it over the dish. It was a weak substitute. But the dish was strong enough to pick up signals from 6,523 **light years** away. The event was called the "first light." That is the moment that brings a telescope to life. Astronomer George Hobbes could hardly believe it. "It's amazing that they could do this with a simple antenna,"[5] he said.

This evening shot taken in late June 2016 gives a colorful view of the FAST Telescope.

Other issues cropped up. Li reported that the **actuators** that control the panels were breaking down at a high rate. Actuators can fail because water leaks in and freezes. Waterproofing can be a problem with vertical telescopes. But it was an easier solution for FAST. Its actuators can be worked on from the ground.

FAST FACT ✏️

Several large radio telescopes were built after World War II ended in 1945. The first was the Lovell Telescope in Manchester, England (shown here). It was the biggest in the world when it was built in 1957. It was outdone five years later by the Green Bank Telescope in West Virginia. Arecibo became the largest in 1963 and remained the most powerful until FAST came along.[6]

Li was not overly worried. He had the working actuators hold part of the dish in a more upright position. It would then be pointed to the sky and catch whatever signals it could as the Earth rotated. The scan would survey the sky for 200 days.

Nan believed that would lead to great discoveries. Included would be as many as 1,000 previously unheard pulsars. That would add to the 2,500 already known. Astronomers could then study the space between stars and galaxies, which would lead to detecting gravitational waves. Radio astronomer Dick Manchester could hardly wait. "They're very close to achieving an absolutely remarkable feat,"[7] he said.

While it was an encouraging start, "very close" was not good enough. It remained to be seen just how well the FAST telescope would perform. Only time would tell what it could accomplish.

And another problem soon began to threaten its abilities. This problem had nothing to do with the telescope itself.

Astronomers hope that FAST will uncover some of the mysteries in far-distant galaxies such as these.

4

The Amazing Attraction

Even though China is the fourth-largest country in the world, many areas of the nation have few residents and even fewer visitors. Among these is Guizhou Province. Few of its attractions have spurred significant tourism.

The construction of the FAST telescope changed that situation. Tourists began flocking to the region soon after the telescope was completed on July 3, 2016. Nearly all of them were Chinese, who were showing support for their country and taking pride in a great achievement. The money they spent added millions of dollars to the local economy. That is a good thing.

It is also a bad thing. The telescope needs clear radio reception and silence to detect signs of alien life and distant pulsars. The vastly increased tourist trade could prevent it from picking up signals from deep space. Many tourists carry cell phones, radios, and digital cameras. The telescope is hindered when they come within three miles of it. A special permit is required to carry such devices to the FAST site. But some visitors ignore the rules. They take photos, send texts, and talk to friends. Many believe that research is needed to determine how many people use such devices within the three-mile radius.

"Since FAST is highly sensitive to the weakest signals from the depths of space, a cellphone being turned on near the site is like shining a flashlight on a human eye that was staring at the stars in

World's largest radio telescope

China's Five-hundred-metre Aperture Spherical Radio Telescope (FAST)

CHINA

GUIZHOU

● Guiyang

FAST ◎

50 km

Mission:

- Observe distant **pulsars** -- tiny neutron stars believed to be the products of supernova explosions

- Survey **neutral hydrogen** in Milky Way, other galaxies

- Search for signs of **alien life**

6 cable-support towers hold receiver in place
Height: 150 m each

Suspended receiver (feed cabin) gathers data from reflector

Cable net structure is connected by more than 7,000 steel wires

4,450 panels
427-483 kg each,
1.3-millimeter-thin

In a test run, FAST detected electromagnetic waves emitted by a pulsar more than 1,300 light-years away

Construction: Started 2011
Some 10,000 people living within 5 km have been relocated

Cost: 1.2 billion yuan ($180 million)

Comparison

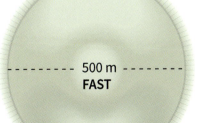

305 m
Arecibo Observatory
Puerto Rico

500 m
FAST

Source : FAST/Chinese Academy of Sciences/National Astronomical Observation/StateMedia

© **AFP**

From its size comparison to the Arecibo Observatory to its construction, cost, various parts and operation, the FAST Telescope detects electromagnetic waves from pulsars and stores information about the stars, galaxies, and possible alien life.

the dead of night. You'll be instantly blinded,"[1] said Zhang Shuxin, FAST deputy manager.

The center of the increased tourism is the town of Kedu. It is just three miles from the telescope and boasts a population of 45,000. In anticipation of the tourist boom, townspeople built dozens of hotels and restaurants to serve the visitors. The centerpiece is an astronomy theme park that occupies more than a square mile. It includes a museum, space-themed hotel, visitor reception facilities, and a learning center that focuses on radio astronomy. The park is aimed at affluent residents of Chinese cities and tickets sell for nearly $100 apiece. The entire complex cost more

The visitor center in Kedu has hosted millions of visitors eager to see the FAST Telescope in person. The center includes a planetarium and other attractions.

than $225 million, which is more money than it took to build the telescope.[2]

The Great Wall of China is the nation's most famous landmark. It attracts more than 10 million visitors every year. According to some reports, the FAST telescope attracted nearly four million visitors in the first half of 2017. A local tourism official anticipated even more people during the rest of the year, perhaps even rising to a total of 10 million. "That will be as many as the tourists to the Great Wall in Beijing," the official said. "Here we have a new wonder of the world."[3]

Attendance peaked during China's Dragon Boat Festival on May 30, when more than 200,000 people descended on the area. That is more than twice the number of visitors to Arecibo in a single year.[4]

The result has created a dilemma. The Guizhou economy is improving because of the telescope. Yet the telescope might lose power because of it. And if it stops working, people will stop coming. The economy will then suffer again.

FAST FACT ✏

The Great Wall of China was built in several sections, starting as early as the 8th century BCE (BEFORE COMMON ERA), and eventually spanning a period of about 2,000 years. The entire wall with all its branches has been measured at 13,171 miles (21,196 kilometers). Some people have claimed that it is visible from space with the naked eye but this is not true.[5]

Experts saw the problem coming. One engineer feared a huge waste of money. The daily operation of the telescope costs $60,000. That adds up to $1.8 million a month and about $22 million a year. That is indeed a lot of money that could go down the drain. But it does not compare to the income the telescope creates. Tourists pumped about $690 million into the local economy by the late summer of 2017. Kedu officials and business owners do not want to give that up.

Yet the telescope was built as far away from human activity as possible to prevent radio interference. Chinese science writer May Chiao noted that. "The scientists do have a valid concern," May said. "Mobile phones signals and WiFi operate at frequencies within the telescope's operating

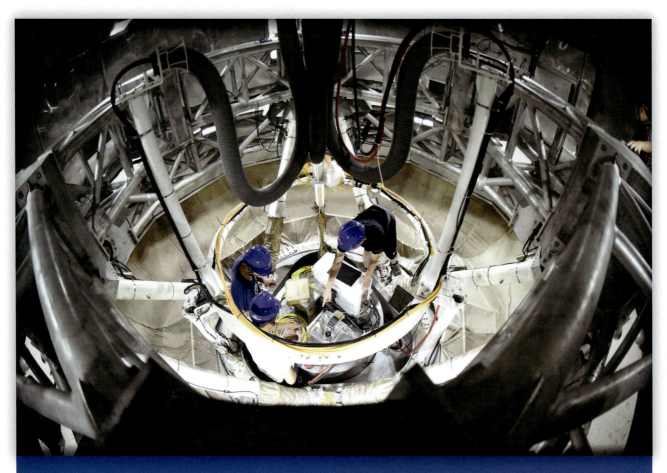

Two workers are seen here in the feedback source cabin of the FAST Telescope in August, 2017.

range. So phones would interfere with the faint signals that the scientists are trying to detect from the edge of the cosmos."[6]

In 2015, Nan stated his fear that even planes flying overhead would be a problem. When they send messages to the ground many miles away, it is like an electronic storm for the telescope.

Any interference is a problem. The FAST telescope has shown great range. Its potential to find alien life grows with every extra light year in its power to receive. So is answering the mystery of how the universe started.

That effort has been weighed against the desire for tourism money. Some feel that gaining knowledge takes priority. Others claim that helping people in one of the poorest provinces in China is far more important. "There may not be an easy solution and may require compromise from both sides,"[7] pointed out Zhu Jin, director of the Beijing Planetarium.

Only time will tell if the conflict can be resolved. It appears that the battle between money and science will not end anytime soon.

FAST FACT ✏

It does not take much to ruin a signal. The Parkes radio telescope in Australia had been detecting a strange signal since 1998. It took 17 years to figure out the source. It was coming from the microwave in the break room of the facility![8]

An Incredible Feat

Before he died in September, 2017, Rendong Nan stated that he was not very interested in science. That was a strange claim coming from the man who was both the chief scientist and chief engineer of the FAST telescope. It is especially evident in the latter area that he proved his genius. The telescope is considered a marvel of engineering.

Fred Lo, the former director of the U.S. National Radio Astronomy Observatory, was stunned by the design and construction of the telescope. "As a civil engineering feat, FAST is obviously amazing,"[1] he said.

Just how amazing it performs is still unknown. It has received great hype. But it will be compared to two other eyes in the sky: the Arecibo telescope and the Square Kilometer Array (SKA).

FAST and Arecibo are similar. Both lie in crater-like depressions that fit their shapes. Both dishes can only look straight up. Both depend on the rotation of the Earth to view various parts of the sky. Both feature shifting detectors suspended over the center of the dish.

That is where the similarities end. FAST is bigger and stronger than Arecibo. Its unique system of cables and **pulleys** allows it to position itself to scan much more area in space. It has more than twice the data-collecting area. It can study fainter and more distant objects.

This photo shows the feed antenna of the Arecibo Radio Telescope in Puerto Rico. Its dish reflector was constructed within a valley in the landscape with the feed antenna that steers the telescope suspended by cables. The dome shields the feed antenna from interference. The inset image shows

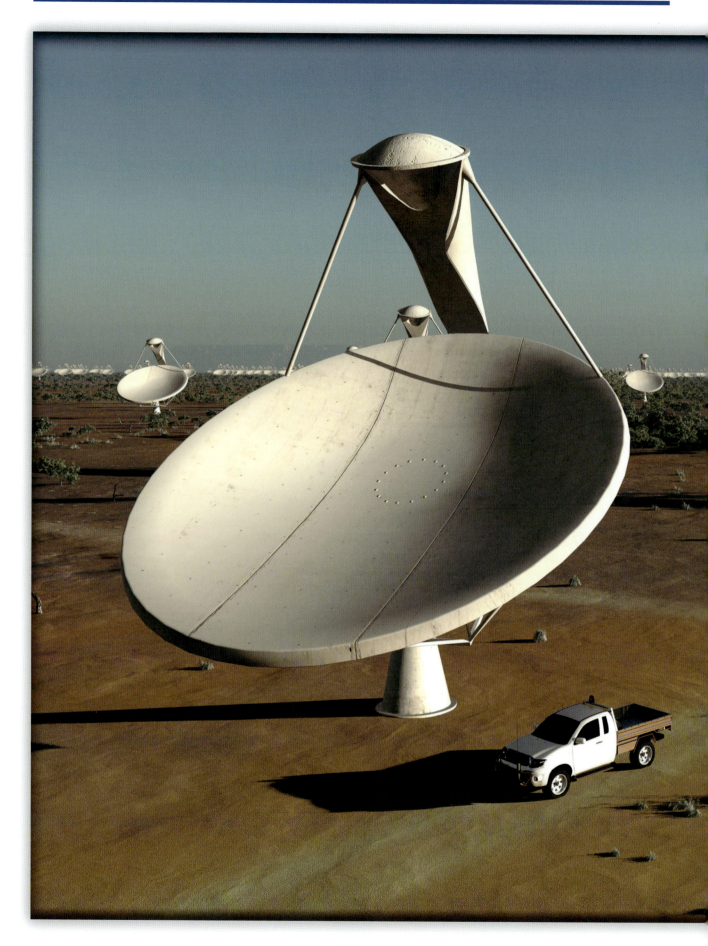

An artist's impression of the Australian Square Kilometer Array radio telescope project. The SKA was a joint award to Australia and South Africa.

Science Matters

The new age of giants

Plans to build the world's largest radio telescope are moving ahead, along with projects to build two more new giant science instruments.

Square Kilometer Array

Construction start 2016

Thousands of coordinated radio dishes centered on site in southern Africa or Australia

Total effective antenna area 0.39 sq. mi. (1 sq. km)

Radio waves from distant stars, galaxies

Webb Space Telescope

Will orbit sun staying 1 million mi. (1.5 million km) from Earth

Will collect infrared light with cooled detectors

Launch 2014 or later

21 ft. (6.5-meter) mirror

Sun shade

European Extremely Large Telescope

138 ft. (42 m) diameter mirror; to be built in Chile

Completion 2018

Source: European Space Agency, NASA, Jodrell Bank Observatory
Graphic: Helen Lee McComas © 2011 MCT

Comparing the FAST to SKA projects is like comparing apples to oranges. They have little in common. SKA is not one structure. It will consist of up to 2,000 upright dishes and one million antennas after construction begins in 2018. FAST has taken the lead in radio telescope technology. It will remain the greatest marvel of telescope engineering in the world. But it is not in competition with SKA.

Chinese astronomers are expected to receive top priority on FAST for about two years. Then it will be opened to scientists around the world. The SKA project also has an international flavor, in which China is a full partner.[2]

FAST FACT

The FAST telescope scientists can thank Australia for its data system. It was developed by the International Centre for Radio Astronomy, based in Perth. The Next Generation Archive System will help astronomers using FAST to collect, move, and store information.[5]

Though China lost out in its bid to host the SKA, it will play a huge role in the project. Its **supercomputers** will process scans of distant stars and galaxies from SKA. They will then turn them over to be analyzed and studied by astronomers around the world.[3] Andreas Wicenec studies data for the International Centre for Radio Astronomy Research. He is excited about what the Chinese supercomputer will do. "It is known as the SKA Science Data Processor," he said. "(It is) the 'brain' of the telescope."[4]

The Square Kilometer Array will eventually overtake FAST in collecting space data. It boasts a total collecting area about four times larger. SKA also features incredible imaging abilities.

Just as China is contributing to SKA, the international astronomy community is contributing to FAST. The Chinese telescope will use the Next Generation Archive System to help store and maintain its findings. It will be aided by the European Southern Observatory.

They are all working on the same side. The goal of both FAST and SKA is to help solve mysteries. Humankind will benefit if either of them can detect alien life on a distant planet or solve the age-old question about how the universe was formed.

Perhaps the FAST Telescope will never find living beings elsewhere. Perhaps it will never discover how the universe got started. But it is trying to quench a thirst for knowledge.

Scientists have been hoping to solve the great mysteries for thousands of years. FAST has strengthened that quest. And the telescope is more than an eye to the sky. It is also one of the greatest engineering feats in history.

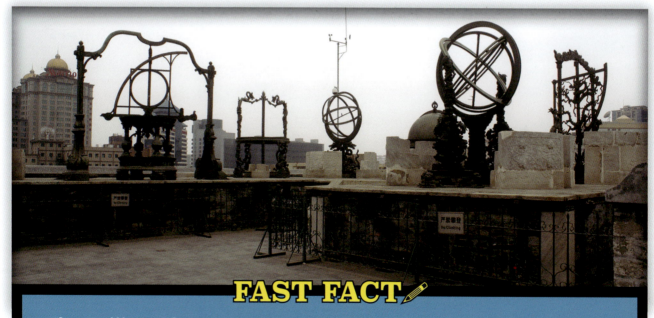

FAST FACT 🖉

The Beijing Observatory was built in the 1400s. But many of its instruments were created more than 200 years later by European missionary Ferdinand Verbiest. Verbiest was placed in charge of the observatory in 1673. He used knowledge gained in Europe to build the instruments. He also used Asian symbolism and images.[6]

WHAT YOU SHOULD KNOW

⭐ FAST cost $180 million to build.

⭐ About 9,000 people living within three miles of the site were forced out of their homes to avoid interfering with incoming radio waves.

⭐ The dish has 4,450 panels.

⭐ The dish is 500 meters (1,640 feet) in diameter.

⭐ It surpassed the Arecibo Telescope in Puerto Rico as the largest radio telescope in the world.

⭐ The telescope is located in Guizhou Province in southeast China.

⭐ The dish was placed in a crater-like depression for an ideal fit.

⭐ Construction of the structure began in 2011 and was completed on July 3, 2016.

⭐ A mesh of steel ropes allows the dish to point at certain spots in space.

⭐ The remote area in China was among the 400 spots Chinese scientists studied over a 10-year period. The valley selected was considered an ideal size. The surrounding mountains provided a shield against radio interference.

⭐ It allows scientists to detect dense, rotating stars called pulsars.

⭐ Ripples in space and time called gravitational waves detected by the telescope could help scientists learn how galaxies evolved.

⭐ Scientists believe that FAST is 5-10 times more likely to discover alien life on distant planets than other telescopes.

⭐ China placed a bid to host the Square Kilometer Array, but lost out to Australia and South Africa. It then went ahead with the FAST project instead.

⭐ Many hotels and restaurants have been built around the telescope to serve curious visitors.

⭐ The telescope was first proposed in 1994. It was not approved by the Chinese government until 13 years later.

⭐ Its receivers can be steered to cover about twice the width of sky than the Arecibo telescope.

⭐ Rendong Nan, the chief scientist and chief engineer on the FAST Telescope project, spoke on astronomy as a guest lecturer in many countries.

⭐ The system that pulls a section nearly 1,000 feet in diameter has been described as a bowl inside a wok.

⭐ Due to its strength, FAST can study more faint and distant objects in space than any other single-dish telescope.

⭐ The telescope is expected to help support the growing Chinese space program.

QUICK STATS

⭐ Diameter: 500 meters (1,640 feet)
⭐ Number of panels: 4,450
⭐ Construction cost: $180 million

⭐ Length of construction: 5 years
⭐ Size of movable system: 984 feet

1609   Italian physicist Galileo Galilei builds the first telescope and uses it to discover the four largest moons of Jupiter, detect sunspots on the surface of the sun, and observe craters on Mars.

1655   Dutch astronomer Christiaan Huygens builds the most powerful telescope to date and views planets in our solar system.

1789   Astronomer William Herschel builds the first giant reflector telescope.

1897   American astronomer Alvan Clark builds the world's largest refracting telescope—the Yerkes Telescope in Wisconsin.

1932   Karl Jansky of Bell Telephone Laboratories detects radio waves from the Milky Way.

1937   American engineer Grote Reber creates the first radio telescope.

1957   The Mullard Radio Astronomy Observatory opens in Cambridge, England.

1994   The FAST Telescope is first proposed.

2007   The Chinese government approves the project.

2008   The foundation-laying ceremony takes place at the work site.

2011   Construction begins on the FAST Telescope, forcing more than 9,000 people out of their homes.

2016   The last panel is placed; the first light is achieved without an active reflector.

2017   The telescope site becomes a tourist attraction.

Chapter 1—Big Hope for a Big Telescope

1. "What are Radio Telescopes?" National Radio Astronomy Observatory. https://public.nrao.edu/telescopes/radio-telescopes/

2. Katie Hunt, "China's giant space telescope starts search for alien life." CNN. September 21, 2016. http://www.cnn.com/2016/09/21/health/china-fast-telescope-search-for-aliens/index.html

3. Ibid.

4. Jesse Emspak, "Does the universe have an edge?" Live Science. June 2, 2016. https://www.livescience.com/33646-universe-edge.html

5. Dennis Normile, "World's largest radio telescope will search for dark matter, listen for aliens." *Science Magazine*. September 26, 2016. http://www.sciencemag.org/news/2016/09/world-s-largest-radio-telescope-will-search-dark-matter-listen-aliens

6. Hunt, "China's giant space telescope starts search for alien life."

7. Deborah Byrd, "Alien seekers report 15 more fast radio bursts." *EarthSky*. September 2, 2017. http://earthsky.org/space/fast-radio-bursts-repeating-frb-121102-breakthrough-listen

8. Hunt, "China's giant space telescope starts search for alien life."

Chapter 2—Birth of a Marvel

1. "Rendong Nan." National Astronomical Observatories of China: Chinese Academy of Sciences. http://sourcedb.naoc.cas.cn/en/enaoexpert/200907/t20090706_2000371.html

2. Anil Ananthaswamy, "China starts building world's biggest radio telescope." New Scientist. June 8, 2011. https://www.newscientist.com/article/mg21028165-300-china-starts-building-worlds-biggest-radio-telescope/

3. Dennis Normile, "World's largest radio telescope will search for dark matter, listen for aliens." *Science Magazine*. September 26, 2016. http://www.sciencemag.org/news/2016/09/world-s-largest-radio-telescope-will-search-dark-matter-listen-aliens

4. "What is karst? And why is it important?" Karst Waters Institute. https://karstwaters.org/educational-resources/what-is-karst-and-why-is-it-important/

5. Dennis Normile, "World's largest radio telescope will search for dark matter, listen for aliens."

6. Katie Hunt, "China's giant space telescope starts search for alien life." CNN. September 21, 2016. http://www.cnn.com/2016/09/21/health/china-fast-telescope-search-for-aliens/index.html

7. Becky Davis, "Thousands displaced for China's huge telescope." Yahoo! News. November 30, 2016. https://www.yahoo.com/news/thank-aliens-thousands-displaced-chinas-huge-telescope-063846215.html

8. Ibid.

9. Cecille De Jesus, "The quest for life beyond earth: The world's largest radio telescope just went online." Futurism. September 26, 2016. https://futurism.com/the-quest-for-life-beyond-earth-the-worlds-largest-radio-telescope-just-went-online/

10. Jennifer Pak, "Thousands to be relocated in China to make way for world's largest radio telescope." *The Telegraph*. February 17, 2016. http://www.telegraph.co.uk/news/worldnews/asia/china/12161281/Thousands-to-be-relocated-in-China-to-make-way-for-worlds-largest-radio-telescope.html

11. Normile, "World's largest radio telescope will search for dark matter, listen for aliens."

Chapter 3—Bigger and Stronger

1. Edward Wong, "Chinese Telescope to Displace 9,000 Villagers in Hunt for Extraterrestrials. *New York Times*, February 17, 2016. https://www.nytimes.com/2016/02/18/world/asia/china-fast-telescope-guizhou-relocation.html

2. Dennis Normile, "World's largest radio telescope will search for dark matter, listen for aliens." *Science Magazine*. September 26, 2016. http://www.sciencemag.org/news/2016/09/world-s-largest-radio-telescope-will-search-dark-matter-listen-aliens

3. Drago Mitrica, "China is building the world's largest radio telescope – and it's almost done." ZME Science. October 6, 2015. http://www.zmescience.com/science/astronomy/china-telescope-radio-06102015/

4. Dennis Normile, "World's largest radio telescope will search for dark matter, listen for aliens."

5. Ibid.

6. Renjiang Xie, "Big developments in Chinese astronomy." *Sky and Telescope*. January 21, 2009. http://www.skyandtelescope.com/astronomy-news/big-developments-in-chinese-astronomy/

7. Ibid.

Chapter 4—An Amazing Attraction

1. Zhou Chen and Wu Gang, "China fires up world's biggest radio telescope—but selfies could jam its hunt for aliens." Marketwatch.com, September 27, 2016, http://www.marketwatch.com/story/china-fires-up-worlds-biggest-radio-telescope-but-selfies-could-jam-its-hunt-for-aliens-2016-09-26

2. Becky Davis, "Thousands displaced for China's huge telescope." Yahoo! News, November 30, 2016. https://www.yahoo.com/news/thank-aliens-thousands-displaced-chinas-huge-telescope-063846215.html

3. Stephen Chen, "How noisy Chinese tourists may be drowning out interstellar signals at the world's biggest telescope." *South China Morning Post*, August 24, 2017. http://www.businessinsider.com/chinese-tourist-disrupt-fast-signals-worlds-biggest-telescope-2017-8

4. Ibid.

5. Melanie Lieberman, "17 secrets of the Great Wall of China." *Travel + Leisure*. April 20, 2017. http://www.travelandleisure.com/travel-tips/the-great-wall-of-china

6. Wang Lianzhang, "World's largest telescope at risk from tourists' smartphones." Sixth Tone. September 26, 2016. http://www.sixthtone.com/news/1380/world%20s-largest-telescope-no-match-tourists%20-smartphones

7. Chen, "Noisy Chinese tourists."

8. Monica Tan, "Microwave oven to blame for mystery signal that left astronomers stumped." *The Guardian*. May 5, 2015. https://www.theguardian.com/science/2015/may/05/microwave-oven-caused-mystery-signal-plaguing-radio-telescope-for-17-years

Chapter 5—An Incredible Feat

1. Dennis Normile, "World's largest radio telescope will search for dark matter, listen for aliens." *Science Magazine*. September 26, 2016. http://www.sciencemag.org/news/2016/09/world-s-largest-radio-telescope-will-search-dark-matter-listen-aliens

2. Katie Hunt, "China's giant space telescope starts search for alien life." CNN. September 21, 2016. http://www.cnn.com/2016/09/21/health/china-fast-telescope-search-for-aliens/index.html 3. "World's biggest telescope meets world's second fastest supercomputer." International Centre for Radio Astronomy Research. August 22, 2016. https://www.icrar.org/tianhe2/

4. Ibid.

5. ICRAR, "Australian technology installed on world's largest single-dish radio telescope." September 26, 2016. https://www.icrar.org/fast/

6. China Highlights. Beijing Ancient Observatory—One of the Oldest in the World. https://www.chinahighlights.com/beijing/attraction/beijing-ancient-observatory.htm

Aguilar, David A. *Alien Worlds: Your Guide to Extraterrestrial Life*. Washington, D.C.: National Geographic for Kids, 2013.

——. *Space Encyclopedia: A Tour of Our Solar System and Beyond*. Washington, D.C.: National Geographic for Kids, 2013.

Blake, Mark and Jack Colin. *Alien Hunter's Handbook: How to Look for Extra-Terrestrial Life*. New York: Kingfisher Books, 2013.

Jill McDonald, Jill. *Hello World! Solar System*. New York: Doubleday Books for Young Readers, 2016.

Read, John. *50 Things to See With a Telescope*. Seattle, WA: Amazon Digital Services, 2017.

WORKS CONSULTED

Ananthaswamy, Anil. "China starts building world's biggest radio telescope." New Scientist. June 8, 2011. https://www.newscientist.com/article/mg21028165-300-china-starts-building-worlds-biggest-radio-telescope/

Byrd, Deborah. "Alien seekers report 15 more fast radio bursts." EarthSky. September 2, 2017. http://earthsky.org/space/fast-radio-bursts-repeating-frb-121102-breakthrough-listen

Chen, Stephen. "How noisy Chinese tourists may be drowning out interstellar signals at the world's biggest telescope." *South China Morning Post*, August 24, 2017. http://www.businessinsider.com/chinese-tourist-disrupt-fast-signals-worlds-biggest-telescope-2017-8

China Highlights. Beijing Ancient Observatory—One of the Oldest in the World. https://www.chinahighlights.com/beijing/attraction/beijing-ancient-observatory.htm

Davis, Becky. "Thousands displaced for China's huge telescope." Yahoo! News. November 30, 2016. https://www.yahoo.com/news/thank-aliens-thousands-displaced-chinas-huge-telescope-063846215.html

De Jesus, Cecilia. "The quest for life beyond earth: The world's largest radio telescope just went online." Futurism. September 26, 2016. https://futurism.com/the-quest-for-life-beyond-earth-the-worlds-largest-radio-telescope-just-went-online/

Emspak, Jesse. "Does the universe have an edge?" Live Science. June 2, 2016. https://www.livescience.com/33646-universe-edge-html

"History of astronomy in China." International Dunhuang Project. http://idp.bl.uk/4DCGI/education/astronomy/history.html

Hunt, Katie. "China's giant space telescope starts search for alien life." CNN. September 21, 2016. http://www.cnn.com/2016/09/21/health/china-fast-telescope-search-for-aliens/index.html

Karst Waters Institute. "What is karst? And why is it important?" https://karstwaters.org/educational-resources/what-is-karst-and-why-is-it-important/

Lianzhang, Wang. "World's largest telescope at risk from tourists' smartphones." Sixth Tone. September 26, 2016. http://www.sixthtone.com/news/1380/world%20s-largest-telescope-no-match-tourists%20-smartphones

Lieberman, Melanie. "17 secrets of the Great Wall of China." *Travel + Leisure*. April 20, 2017. http://www.travelandleisure.com/travel-tips/the-great-wall-of-china

Mitrica, Drago. "China is building the world's largest radio telescope – and it's almost done." ZME Science. October 6, 2015. http://www.zmescience.com/science/astronomy/china-telescope-radio-06102015/

Normile, Dennis. "World's largest radio telescope will search for dark matter, listen for aliens." *Science Magazine*. September 26, 2016. http://www.sciencemag.org/news/2016/09/world-s-largest-radio-telescope-will-search-dark-matter-listen-aliens

Pak, Jennifer. "Thousands to be relocated in China to make way for world's largest radio telescope." *The Telegraph*. February 17, 2016. http://www.telegraph.co.uk/news/worldnews/asia/china/12161281/Thousands-to-be-relocated-in-China-to-make-way-for-worlds-largest-radio-telescope.html

"Rendong Nan." National Astronomical Observatories of China: Chinese Academy of Sciences. http://sourcedb.naoc.cas.cn/en/enaoexpert/200907/t20090706_2000371.html

Tan, Monica. "Microwave oven to blame for mystery signal that left astronomers stumped." *The Guardian*. May 5, 2015. https://www.theguardian.com/science/2015/may/05/microwave-oven-caused-mystery-signal-plaguing-radio-telescope-for-17-years

"What are Radio Telescopes?" National Radio Astronomy Observatory. https://public.nrao.edu/telescopes/radio-telescopes/

Wong, Edward. "Chinese Telescope to Displace 9,000 Villagers in Hunt for Extraterrestrials. *New York Times*, February 17, 2016. https://www.nytimes.com/2016/02/18/world/asia/china-fast-telescope-guizhou-relocation.html

"World's biggest telescope meets world's second fastest supercomputer." International Centre for Radio Astronomy Research. August 22, 2016. https://www.icrar.org/tianhe2/

Xie, Renjiang. "Big developments in Chinese astronomy." *Sky and Telescope*. January 21, 2009. http://www.skyandtelescope.com/astronomy-news/big-developments-in-chinese-astronomy/

ON THE INTERNET

Five-Hundred-Meter Aperture Spherical Radio Telescope
    http://fast.bao.ac.cn/en/
Kids Astronomy
    https://www.kidsastronomy.com/
Amazing Space
    http://amazingspace.org
Space Scoop
    http://www.spacescoop.org/en/

actuator (AK-choo-a-ter)—device that supplies and transmits energy for another mechanism

alien (A-lee-uhn)— being from outside of the planet Earth

aperture (AP-er-cher)—a hole or small opening

astronomy (uh-STRAHN-uh-mee)—the study of space

axis (AK-sis)—an imaginary straight line around which something turns

depression (dee-PRESH-uhn)—an area on a surface that is lower than other parts

galaxies (GAL-uhk-seez)—large groups of stars that are part of the universe

gravitational wave (grav-i-TAY-shun-uhl WAVE)—a wave of energy produced by fast-moving masses in space

interference (in-ter-FEER-uhnts)—something that gets in the way and prevents something else from working properly

light year (LITE YEER)—the distance that light travels in one year, about 5.9 trillion miles (9.5 trillion kilometers)

pulley (PUHL-ee)—wheel or set of wheels used with a rope or chain to lift or lower heavy objects

pulsar (PUHL-sahr)—type of star that emits rapidly repeating radio waves

supercomputer (soo-per-kuhm-PYOO-ter)—a large and very fast computer

winch (WINCH)—machine with rope or chain used for pulling or lifting heavy things

ABOUT THE AUTHOR

Marty Gitlin is an educational book author based in Cleveland, Ohio. He has published 120 books since 2006. He won numerous awards in 11 years as a newspaper journalist, including first place for general excellence from the Associated Press. That organization also selected him as one of the top four feature writers in Ohio.